OUT OF THE BOX

AMAZING
CARD TRICKS
FROM A SEALED PACK

STUART LEE

OUT OF THE BOX

AMAZING
CARD TRICKS
FROM A SEALED PACK

ALL YOU NEED
TO KNOW

Order this book online at www.trafford.com
or email orders@trafford.com

Most Trafford titles are also available at major online book retailers.

Printed in the United States of America.

ISBN: 978-1-4669-4588-3 (sc)
ISBN: 978-1-4669-4589-0 (e)

Library of Congress Control Number: 2012911741

Trafford rev. 08/10/2012

 www.trafford.com

North America & International
toll-free: 1 888 232 4444 (USA & Canada)
phone: 250 383 6864 ♦ fax: 812 355 4082

CONTENTS

INTRODUCTION

ALTHOUGH AT A VERY young age, like most other children, I had been delighted and intrigued by so-called "magic" tricks, particularly those involving playing cards, at no time had I shown anything more than a passing interest in performing them myself. However, as the years went by, having witnessed a particularly striking performance of a trick, I would be sufficiently enthused to find out how it had been done. Thus, over time, I acquired the ability to perform a few very simple tricks with an ordinary pack of cards and some more impressive ones with the aid of specially prepared packs.

On some high days and holidays, I could be encouraged by friends to show off one or more of these tricks. They were a most accommodating audience. In fact, I suspect that on most occasions they were as aware as I was of how the effect was being achieved. Nevertheless, a trick (however simple) is always intriguing and they encouraged me.

What converted this spasmodic and moderate interest in card magic into an almost all-consuming pursuit was a combination of circumstances some ten Christmases ago. I had retired from a long career in the Army some years before and therefore I then had the time and opportunity to indulge all my hobbies and interests. On that particular Christmas my wife and I were staying in Northumberland with my wife's sister and her husband and to keep me amused they presented me with a book of puzzles, games and tricks. The contents more than lived up to the title: "*The Curious Book of Mind-Boggling Tricks, Puzzles and Games*" (Charles Barry Townsend, Sterling Publishing Co. Inc., New York). Although the puzzles and games certainly kept me amused, it was the card tricks that particularly attracted my attention. Most of them I had already come across before in one form or another but some of them were new to me. In any event, I had the time over the Christmas holiday to give to each of them a little more attention than I had when I had come across them before. The result was that I spent that Christmas and a few weeks after it pondering on how they might be developed and improved.

While doing so I began to search my local lending libraries and bookshops for anything I could find on card magic and it soon became apparent from the references and bibliographies that I found in the books I came across that there was a wealth of material available. I determined therefore to acquire a basic reference library that would enable me to become acquainted with a whole spectrum of card tricks and routines and the skills and sleights-of-hand associated with them. As it might spare the reader many hours of searching out such books for him- or herself the results of my forays in the bookshops are set out here.

The first acquisition was "*The Royal Road to Card Magic*" by Jean Hugard and Frederick Braué (Dover Publications Inc., New York, 1999), which proved to be a most useful introduction to a range of basic card manipulations and tricks involving these skills. This was followed by the book "*Expert Card Technique*" (Dover Publications Inc., New York, 1974) by the same authors, which guides the reader through more complicated techniques and effects. Next Hugard's "*Encyclopaedia of Card Tricks*" (Dover Publications Inc., New York, 1974 and Foulsham, Slough, 2003) proved to be a veritable cornucopia of information not only on the card tricks themselves but also of the underlying principles and specialist and pre-prepared packs. It also includes a brief guide to the performance of a number of basic sleights-of-hand and a description of "*The Nikola Card System*" for memorising the order of the cards in a pack.

These three books alone were more than enough to satisfy my requirements for a basic reference library, but, as with most interests, the more I studied them the more I wanted more information on particular aspects of card magic. The first was the ways in which the principles of mathematics could be applied to handling and ordering the cards. Again, I found that there was no lack of material, but there were two books that particularly attracted my attention: Arthur F. MacTier's "*Card Concepts*" (Davenport, London, 2000) and Martin Gardner's "*Mathematics, Magic, and Mystery*" (Dover Publications Inc., New York, 1956). The former is a most comprehensive review of what the author describes in the book's subtitle as the "numerical and sequential principles within card magic". It also gives detailed descriptions of tricks with cards using these principles. Finally, it provides a wealth of information on other authors, sources, and references in the field. Martin Gardner's book describes not only tricks with cards but also a variety of other effects that can be produced by applying mathematical principles.

The second area of card magic that attracted my particular attention was that of the systems that could be used to memorise the order of the cards in a pre-arranged pack. "*The Nikola Card System*" referred to above is one, but there are many more. Juan Tamariz's book "*Mnemonica*" (Hermetic Press Inc., Seattle, 2004), although concentrating on his own "ultra-rapid" system and the many effects that can be produced from it, also describes and gives references for most of the other systems that have been developed, eg "The Rosary Deck", "The Eight Kings System", "The Si Stebbins Stack", etc. However, after much research and personal experimentation, the system I found to be the most suited to my purposes and also easy to master was that set out in the book "*The Osterlind Breakthrough Card System*" (Osterlind Mysteries, 2004) by Richard Osterlind. Although this system is not designed to allow you to memorise the order of the cards in the pre-arranged pack it does allow you immediately to identify any given card from the identity of either the preceding or following card in the pack.

My next area of interest was those tricks in card magic described as "self-working". I soon found that one author in particular, Karl Fulves, had concentrated his attention on such tricks and his books (all published by Dover Publications Inc., New York) were added to my ever-growing library: "*Self-Working Card Tricks*" (1974), "*More Self-Working Card Tricks*" (1984), "*Self-Working Close-Up Card Magic*" (1995) and, for the card tricks included, "*Self-Working Mental Magic*" (1979).

Having collected together all this material I settled down to study it. I worked through the descriptions of the tricks and noted those that produced the most spectacular effects. I amended them, where it seemed appropriate, and, in some cases, using the principles involved in one trick I developed another with what I considered to be a more impressive outcome. I practised the sleights-of-hand and, where I could, simplified and, hopefully, improved the handling of the cards. Finally, I began to put together sequences of tricks into routines that allowed one trick to follow naturally from and build on the trick that preceded it.

It was at this point that I came to the conclusion that what would help me to remember the tricks and allow me to present them in the most effective way was a carefully thought-through structured sequence of routines set out in a note-book that I could use to give me an overview of the sequences and allow me, from time to time, to refresh my memory on the handling and presentation of a particular trick. Once completed I found it an indispensable tool in learning and retaining the mechanics of the tricks and it occurred to me that with some additional background information it could prove to be as useful to others as it was for me. On this basis I produced my first book on card magic "*Old Wine In A New Bottle*" (Trafford, Bloomington, 2010). My aim was to produce a practical hand-book that would guide the beginner in card magic through the basic handling of the cards to the successful production of the tricks. I included in it not only detailed descriptions of the working of the tricks but also advice on presentation and full explanations of the techniques that can be used to manipulate and control the cards. All this was set in the context of a routine based on "classic" tricks reworked to produce sometimes new, sometimes stronger, outcomes.

I followed this with a second book "*Magic Aces*" (Trafford, Bloomington, 2011) which, in addition to the basic information on the handling and manipulation of the cards, sets out a routine of tricks in which the Aces of the pack are produced in a variety of novel and spectacular ways. This third book follows the same formula, based on a routine of tricks performed with the cards taken straight from the sealed carton.

Full instructions are given for the performance of the routine, which lasts for approximately 15 minutes. However, it can be extended, if required, by adding tricks from the chapter "*Additional Tricks*".

All the tricks can be performed using the minimum manipulation of the cards and, although variations of the tricks using sleights-of-hand are described, they can be performed without them and detailed instructions for such performance are set out.

In the books "*Old Wine In A New Bottle*" and "*Magic Aces*" it was necessary to begin with definitions of the terms used in describing the cards and in describing the handling of the cards. These are reproduced below.

All 52 cards together are *the pack* or *the deck*

Any part of the pack is *a packet*

A hand (of cards) is a packet that has been dealt to or given to a spectator

To deal consecutively is to deliver to each hand in turn one card until the deal is completed. *To deal the hands individually* is to deliver all the cards required to one hand before proceeding to deal the next hand.

To count cards reversing their order is to place each card as it is counted on top of the previous card. *To count cards without reversing their order* is to place each card as it is counted beneath the previous card.

Face-down and *face-up* cards are self-evident terms, the face of a card being its value and suit.

The long edge of a card, packet, or pack is *the side*.

The short edge of a card, packet, or pack is *the end*.

Front and *forward* and *outward* are away from you, and *rear* and *backward* and *inward* are towards you.

Left and *right* are from your viewpoint.

With the end of the cards or pack pointing towards the spectators, *the outer end* is the end pointing towards the spectators, and *the inner end* is the end pointing towards you.

With the cards or pack held in the right hand and with the outer end pointing towards the spectators, the outer side is to the right and the inner side is towards the left. Similarly, if the outer side is pointing towards the spectators the outer end is to the right and the inner end is to the left.

With the cards or pack held in the left hand and the outer end pointing towards the spectators the outer side is to the left and the inner side is to the right. Similarly, if the outer side is pointing towards the spectators the outer end is to the left and the inner end is to the right.

The fingers are: *first* (or *index*), *second*, *third* (or *ring*), and *fourth* (or *little*, sometimes referred to as "*the pinky*").

To cut and complete is to take a packet of cards from the top of the pack and to place what was the bottom of the pack on top of it. With the cards in hand the same outcome is achieved by *the undercut*, where the bottom part of the pack is cut away and transferred to the top of the pack.

To cull is to extract a card or cards (either openly or secretly) from the rest of the cards in a pack or packet.

An *out-jogged* or *up-jogged* card or packet is a card or packet positioned in the pack so that the card or packet projects from the pack.

A break is a small gap or opening formed secretly within a packet or pack at either the inner end or at the inner corner of the inner side. The former is held by the tip of the thumb of the hand holding the cards and the latter by the tip of the little finger of the hand holding the cards (and for this reason it is sometimes referred to as "*a pinky break*").

A bridged card is a card that has been subjected to pressure either at the sides or the ends to produce a curve along its length or across its width. A forward curve to the face of a card is a *convex bridge*, and a rearward curve to the face of a card is a *concave bridge*.

A few concluding words of advice for the beginner in card magic:

> Study the descriptions of the handling and presentation carefully before you attempt to perform them.

> Go through the manipulations and presentation slowly on the first attempts.

> Try not to look at your hands when shuffling or performing a manipulation.

> Perform the manipulations and presentations over and over again in practice and perform a trick

for others only when you are totally confident of your ability to do so successfully.

If necessary, distract the attention of the spectators away from the cards by diverting their attention elsewhere. This can be done by talking to them directly and requiring a response or by giving them something to do or to look at.

Do not be afraid when the occasion requires it to perform some manipulations openly. It is surprising what can go unnoticed provided it is done boldly and the attention of the spectators distracted by directing it elsewhere.

When you are performing a trick do not rush the presentation. You know the trick and the effect you are attempting, but, hopefully, it is the first time the spectators have seen the trick performed and to rush the presentation would be to confuse them.

As a general rule, never repeat a trick in the same performance. Exceptions are where the same effect or outcome can be achieved by different means or when the mechanics of the trick are such that it is impossible for the spectators to determine how the effect is brought about.

And **never ever** reveal how an effect has been achieved.

THE CARDS

IT MIGHT WELL BE said that performers of card magic are spoiled for choice by the variety of playing cards available to them. There are giant-sized cards and miniature cards, triangular cards, and circular cards. They have plain backs in a full spectrum of colours or patterned backs in as many styles and designs as there are manufacturers. However, the majority of performers prefer to use either the "*Poker-size*" card or the "*Bridge-size*" card, the former being the larger of the two sizes.

A popular example of the Poker-size pack of cards is the "*Bicycle Rider Back*" pack produced by the U.S. Playing Card Co. It has two indexes on the face of each card (ie, the value and suit of each card are shown at the top left and at the bottom right corners) and it can be obtained in a variety of colours for the backs. Of particular interest to some performers is the fact that the packs can also be obtained with blank-faced, blank-backed, double-faced, double-backed cards, and in a miniature size with red, blue or green backs in a design identical to the full-size packs. Additionally, they are available as specially prepared packs to perform particular tricks and effects.

Examples of the Bridge-size packs are the "*No 1*" pack of the Waddington Playing Card Co. Ltd. (Winning Moves UK Ltd.) and the "*Standard*" playing cards produced and sold by W.H. Smith. They come either Red-backed or Blue-backed and are four-indexed cards with the value and suit of the cards show at all four corners of each card. Waddington also produce a four-indexed "*No 1*" Poker pack.

For completeness it should be noted that W.H. Smith produce and sell miniature "*Patience*" packs in identical back design and colour to their "*Standard*" packs and also a Poker-size pack—this latter pack being a card with two extra-large indexes on the face of the card.

A fourth range of playing cards merits attention and that is the "*Classic*" design produced by the Austrian company Piatnik. They are Bridge-size cards available in back designs in red and blue and also in special packs (ie, blank backs, blank faces, etc.). However, because of their order in the sealed pack they are not suitable for use in the routine described in the chapter "*The Routine*". It should also be noted that the descriptions of the handling set out in the chapter "*The Routine*" assume the use of the "*Bicycle Rider Back*" pack. The handling required for the Waddington "*No 1*" pack and the W.H. Smith "*Standard*" pack are given in the chapter "*Alternative Packs*".

THE ROUTINE

Opening The Pack

Start with the sealed carton of cards on the table. Invite a spectator to remove the wrapping, break the seal, and to take the pack out of the carton. Take the pack from the spectator and remove the Joker cards and any other extraneous cards. In doing so do not disturb the order of the pack.

The sequence of the cards in the "*Bicycle Rider Back*" pack is (when the pack is face-down): Ace to King (Hearts)—Ace to King (Clubs)—King to Ace (Diamonds)—King to Ace (Spades). However, it would be prudent to check the sequencing by examining another pack from the same production run. This precaution applies equally for the alternative packs.

Mixing The Pack

If you do not intend to use a bridge card or sleights-of-hand in the performance of the routine proceed directly to the next section of this chapter, "*Arranging the Pack*". If you are using a bridged card and wish to give the impression to the spectator that you are mixing the pack proceed as described in the next paragraph.

With the Ace of Spades as the bridged card you may allow the spectator or any number of spectators to cut and complete the pack, provided that, finally, you cut the bridged card to the bottom of the pack. Additionally, using the bridged card you may perform a false mix of the pack. (*For details of how to produce the bridged card and how to use the bridged card see the relevant section in the chapter "Handling and Sleights of Hand" and for an explanation of the term "cut and complete" see the "Introduction".*)

Arranging The Pack

If you wish to arrange the pack without using a bridged card begin by stating that it would be as well to make sure that all the 52 cards are there in the pack. Count out the first 13 cards from the top of the face-down pack and place them on the table. Do this without reversing their order, ie, as you count the cards off the pack each card is placed beneath the one or ones already counted. Continue counting off the next 13 cards (again without reversing their order) and place these cards on top of the cards already on the table. Continue counting out the rest of the pack (still not reversing the order of the cards) and when the count is completed pick up the cards from the table and place them on top of the cards in hand.

The sequence of the cards is now: Ace to King (Clubs)—Ace to King (Hearts)—King to Ace (Diamonds)—King to Ace (Spades).

To rearrange the sequence of the cards using the bridged card (Ace of Spades) begin by asking a spectator whether he or she would like to have the top half of the pack or the bottom half. Irrespective of the reply count out the first 26 cards from the top of the face-down pack and place them on the table. Do this without reversing their order as described in the preceding paragraph. You then place the remainder of the pack (without counting them out) by the side of the cards already on the table.

Finally, you instruct the spectator to take the part of
the pack that he or she chose and to place it either at
the top or at the bottom of the other half of the pack.
The spectator may then cut and complete the pack as
many times as wished, provided that, finally, you cut the
bridged card to the bottom of the pack. The sequence of
the cards is then as stated above.

Setting The Pack

State that in order to make sure that the pack is thoroughly mixed you are going to deal it out into four piles.

Deal out the cards from the top of the pack face-down into four piles, placing a card in turn on each pile to give:

Pile 1—Pile 2—Pile 3—Pile 4.

Reconstitute the pack by placing Pile 4 on Pile 3 and then those cards on Pile 2, and then all those cards on Pile 1.

Repeat the procedure described in the two preceding paragraphs one more time.

First Trick:
"Cards And Numbers"

1.   If you are not using a bridged card proceed directly to paragraph 3.

2.   If you are performing the routine using a bridged card (Ace of Spades) you should note that this card is now at the bottom of the pack and you may, therefore, if you wish, allow the spectator to cut and complete the pack, provided that, finally, you cut the bridged card to the bottom of the pack.

3.   Now deal out from the top of the face-down pack two piles of face-down cards—one for the spectator and one for yourself. Deal the first card to the spectator and the second card to yourself and continue to deal, placing a card in turn on each pile until the pack is exhausted.

4.   Now ask the spectator to select any number from 1 to 26.

5.   Once the spectator has selected the number go through your cards (without revealing that you are counting them) to the card represented by the calculation 26 minus the spectator's number plus 1 (or, more conveniently, 27 minus the spectator's selected number). Move this card forward from the rest of the cards so that it projects from the packet for about half its length, but do not disturb its order within the packet. Then place the packet (still face-down) on the table.

6. Instruct the spectator to do exactly the same, moving forward the card at his or her stated number.

7. When the two piles are cards are turned face-up the projecting cards will be of the same value and colour.

8. Push the projecting cards back into their positions in the separate packets, turn both packets face-down, and place your cards on top of the spectator's cards.

9. Again deal out face-down two piles of cards—one for the spectator and one for yourself. Again deal the first card to the spectator and the second card to yourself and continue to deal placing a card in turn on each of the piles until each pile contains 26 cards.

10. State that in order to convince the spectator that the cards are neither marked nor arranged in some way you will choose your card first and then allow the spectator to arrive at a completely arbitrary number for the choice of his or her card.

11. In your own packet of cards go through to the 17th card from the top (again without revealing that your are counting) and display it face-down as described in paragraph 5 above.

12. If you are not using the bridged card proceed directly to paragraph 13. If you are using the bridged card (Ace of Spades) you should note that this card is now the bottom card of the spectator's pile of cards and you may therefore, if you wish, allow the spectator to cut and complete that pile of cards, provided

that, finally, you cut the bridged card to the bottom of the pile.

13. Now allow the spectator to arrive at "a completely arbitrary" number by cutting his or her pile of cards roughly in half. You take the bottom half of the cut and place it on top of your own pile of cards in line with the non-projecting cards. You then invite the spectator to deal off face-down onto the table into a pile the cards he or she has cut off. In doing so he or she should count out the number of cards being dealt. When the dealing and the counting have been completed the spectator should add together the two digits of the number arrived at to produce a single figure "arbitrary" number, (eg, 12 = 1 + 2 = 3). (*Note: If on the count the spectator has cut off less than 10 cards instruct him or her to **deal** off onto the pile additional cards from the top of the pack to take the total to 10 or above. Take the total then arrived at and proceed with the calculation using this total. For example, if the spectator has counted out seven cards he or she then **deals** 10 cards to make a total of 17. The calculation is then 17 = 1 + 7 = 8.*)

14. Instruct the spectator to take the cards he or she has dealt out onto the table and to deal them out from the top of the face-down packet face-down into a pile. When he or she reaches the card indicated by the number calculated at paragraph 13 above he or she should take that card and place it (still face-down) projecting about half-way forward on the other cards. The spectator should then continue

dealing out the other cards of the packet aligning them with the non-projecting cards.

15. When the two piles (the spectators and your own) are turned face-up the two projecting cards will be of the same value and the same colour.

16. Push the two projecting cards back into the separate packets, turn both packets face-down, and place the spectator's cards on top of your packet.

Second Trick:
"Bluff—Double Bluff"

1. If you are not using a bridged card in the performance of the routine proceed directly to paragraph 3.

2. If you are using the bridged card (Ace of Spades) you should note that this card is now the 26th card down in the face-down pack. Tell the spectator that for the next trick you need to divide the pack between the two of you and that usually you are able to cut the pack exactly in half. Cut at the bridged card and count out the cards face-down into a pile in front of the spectator (thus reversing their order). You may, if you wish, appear slightly surprised that you have managed to cut the pack exactly in half. Alternatively, you could have cut slightly above the bridged card in which case you would then count off the additional cards from the other packet to bring the total in the pile to 26. In any case you do not disturb the order of the bottom 26 cards of the pack, which you take as your own packet. Now proceed to paragraph 4.

3. If you are not using a bridged card count off the top 26 cards of the face-down pack face-down into a pile in front of the spectator (thus reversing their order) and retain the bottom half of the pack for yourself (thus not reversing their order).

4. Now instruct the spectator to deal out his or her cards side by side on the table forming two face-down piles—Pile 1 and Pile 2 (ie, he or she deals a card

to Pile 1 first and then the second card to Pile 2 and so on throughout the dealing). You match the dealing with your own cards, producing Pile 3 and Pile 4. At any point in the dealing as the spectator places a card on Pile 1 he or she may call "Bluff", in which case the spectator places that card face-up on Pile 1 and the next card face-down on Pile 2. You then place your 2 cards face-down on your piles and invite the spectator to turn any one of them face-up. When he or she does so the card will match in value the spectator's face-up card. The spectator may also at any point in the dealing as he or she is placing a card on Pile 1 call "Double Bluff", in which case he or she places that card face-down on Pile 1 and the next card face-up on Pile 2. You then place your next two cards face-down on the appropriate piles. When the spectator turns your two cards face-up they will both match in value the spectator's face-up card.

Third Trick:
"Separating The Cards"

1. You now have on the table four piles of cards (Pile 1—Pile 2—Pile 3—Pile 4) with face-up and face-down cards in each pile.

2. There are three possible finishes to the routine. The finish described here gives a separation of the cards by colour after the cards have been shuffled. The second (the separation of the cards by colour with the cards in numerical order) and the third (the separation of the cards by suit in numerical order) are described in the chapter "*Adaptations and Alternative Tricks*".

3. If you wish to conclude the routine with the separation of the cards by colour after they have been shuffled proceed as described below.

4. Pick up each pile of cards separately and turn the face-up cards face-down. This is done by dealing from the top of the packet onto the table, turning the face-up cards face-down as you come to them. (*This reverses the order of the cards in the packet.*)

5. When you have done this for all the piles place Pile 4 on Pile 3, all those cards on Pile 2, and then all those cards on Pile 1.

6. You may now allow the spectator to cut and complete the face-down pack as many times as he or

she wishes. (*For an explanation of the term "cut and complete" see the "Introduction".*)

7. When the spectator has finished his or her cutting take the pack and perform a Charlier Shuffle (*For a description of how to perform this shuffle see the relevant section of the chapter "Handling and Sleights-of-Hand".*) When you have done this turn the pack face-up and invite the spectator to cut again, placing the packet he or she has cut off by the side of the other packet. If the two packets have face-cards of the same colour re-constitute the pack and invite the spectator to cut again. Continue with this procedure until a cut of the pack produces two packets with different coloured face-cards.

8. Take the two parts of the pack, turn them face-down and riffle shuffle them together or, if he or she is able to perform it, you may allow the spectator to perform the riffle shuffle. (*For a description of this shuffle see the relevant section of the chapter "Handling and Sleights-of-Hand".*)

9. Now take the face-down pack and deal it out into two piles on the table in the following way:

    a. Take the first card and place it face-up on the table.

    b. Take the next card and place it face-down on the table by the side of the first card.

    c. Take the third card, turn it face-up and, if it is the same colour as the first card, place it on the same pile face-up and place the next card (the fourth card) face-down on the second pile. If the third is a different colour to the first card place it face-up on the second card and place the fourth card face-down on the first pile.

d.   Continue with this process until you have two piles of cards on the table in which all the face-up cards in one pile are of one colour and all the face-up cards in the other pile are of a different colour.

10.   Pick up each pile in turn and deal it out, turning all the face-down cards face-up as you come to them. They will all be of the same colour as the face-up cards.

(*Note: If so wished, it is possible to repeat the finish by placing any one of the piles produced on the other and then dealing out the cards as described in the section "Setting The Cards" in this chapter. When you have done this, deal out the cards into two piles, place any one on the other, and then proceed as described at paragraphs 9 and 10 above.*)

ALTERNATIVE PACKS

THE MIXING, ARRANGING, AND setting of the pack described in the first three sections of the chapter "*The Routine*" assume that the cards used are a "*Bicycle Rider Back*" pack. With this pack when the cards are removed from the sealed carton and the Joker and extraneous cards are removed the order of the cards from the top in the face-down pack is Ace to King (Hearts), Ace to King (Clubs), King to Ace (Diamonds), and King to Ace (Spades). The W.H. Smith "*Standard*" pack has exactly the same arrangement and the handling required for the mixing, arrangement, and setting of this pack is therefore as described in the first three sections of the chapter "*The Routine*".

The Waddington "*No 1*" pack has a different order in that all the suits in the sequence Hearts, Clubs, Diamonds, Spades are arranged King to Ace. It therefore requires different handling to put the cards into the necessary pre-arrangement for the routine. To do this proceed as follows:

a.   *Mixing The Pack.* If you are not using a bridged card proceed directly to the next paragraph: "*Arranging the Pack*". If you are using a bridged card proceed as described in the section "*Mixing The Pack*" in the chapter "*The Routine*".

b.   *Arranging The Pack.* To re-arrange the pack to the sequence required for the routine proceed as follows:

- State that you need to confirm that all 52 cards are in the pack.

- Deal off from the top of the pack face-down onto the table the first 26 cards, counting them aloud as you do so. In doing this you are reversing the order of the cards.

- Continue the count from "27-52" with the cards in hand. In performing the count do *not* reverse the order of the cards, ie, as you count the cards each card is placed *beneath* the one or ones already counted.

- When the count is completed place the cards from the table on top of the cards in hand.

- The sequence of the pack is now: Ace to King (Clubs), Ace to King (Hearts), King to Ace (Diamonds), King to Ace (Spades), which is the sequence required to perform the routine.

c.   *Setting The Pack.* The pack is set as described at paragraphs 10-13 of the section "*Setting The Pack*" in the chapter "*The Routine*".

ADAPTATIONS

IN PERFORMING THE FINAL trick of the routine *"Separating The Cards"* there are three possible outcomes. The recommended finish of separating the cards by colour after a riffle shuffle is as described at paragraphs 4-10 of the description of the trick *"Separating The Cards"* in the chapter *"The Routine"*. It brings the routine to a satisfactorily strong conclusion. However, it does destroy the sequence of the cards. Therefore, if you wish to extend the routine using one or two tricks described in the next chapter *"Additional Tricks"*, ie *"All In Order"* and *"Same Number—Same Card"*, it would be better to bring the routine to a conclusion using one of the other two finishes which are described below. They are:

a.   Separating the cards by colour with the cards in a numerical order

b.   Separating the cards by suit with the cards in numerical order within the suits.

The descriptions of these finishes continue from the point at which you have brought the second trick of the routine "*Bluff—Double Bluff*" to a conclusion and you now have on the table four piles of cards (1—2—3—4) with face-up and face-down cards in each pile.

Colour And Numerical Order

1. Pick up each pile of cards separately and turn the face-up cards face-down. As the cards must not be reversed within the piles proceed as follows: without turning the pile over take the cards in turn from the bottom of the pile, placing each card in turn on top of the preceding card and turning the face-up cards face-down as you come to them.

2. Having gone through each pile in this way place Pile 4 on Pile 3, and then those cards on Pile 2, and then all those cards on Pile 1.

3. If you are not using a bridged card proceed directly to paragraph 4 below. If you are using a bridged card you may, if you wish, introduce a false mix of the pack at this point. In any case, you should now invite the spectator to cut and complete the pack. You should then cut the pack to place the bridged card (Ace of Spades) to the bottom of the face-down pack. (*For a definition of the term "cut and complete" see the "Introduction" and for details on how to perform a false mix of the pack see the relevant section of the chapter "Handling and Sleights-of-Hand".*)

4. Now deal out face-down 13 cards to the spectator and instruct him or her to deal the cards out into two face-down piles. As he or she does so note to which pile he or she deals first.

5. When the deal is complete you then deal out from the pack the next 13 cards, dealing a card to each pile in turn, beginning your deal onto the pile to which the spectator dealt second (which is the pile to which he or she did **not** deal his or her last card).

6. Having completed your deal you now deal the next 13 cards to the spectator and instruct him or her to deal the cards out in turn onto the two piles, ensuring that he or she deals first to the pile to which you were dealing second (which is the pile to which you did **not** deal your last card).

7. You now complete the procedure by dealing out the last 13 cards onto the piles, again beginning your deal onto the pile to which the spectator dealt second.

8. Having done so, invite the spectator to take away one of the piles, to turn it face-up, and to deal the cards out onto the table. You take the other pile and, keeping it face-down, deal out from the top of the pile cards face-up onto the table. One pile will be configured: "A"—"7" (Hearts), "8"—"K" (Diamonds), "A"—"7" (Diamonds), "8"—"K" (Hearts). The other will be configured in the same way in the sequence Spades, Clubs, Clubs, Spades.

Suits In Numerical Order

1. Pick up each pile of cards separately and turn the face-up cards face-down. This is done by dealing from the top of the pile onto the table, turning the face-up cards face-down as you come to them. (This reverses the order of the cards in the piles.) If you are not using a bridged card proceed directly to paragraph 3.

2. With your left hand pick up Pile 1 (which has the bridged card (Ace of Spades) as its top card). At the same time pick up Pile 4 with your right hand and place Pile 1 on Pile 4. Then with your left hand place either Pile 3 on Pile 2 or Pile 2 on Pile 3 as directed by the spectator. Finally, allow the spectator to determine whether Pile 1/4 is placed on top or beneath Pile 2/3 or 3/2. (*Note: Taking account of the configuration of the pack produced by the spectator's decision it is possible to perform a false mix of the pack at this point except that instead of cutting the bridged card to the bottom of the pack you should allow it to drop onto the bottom portion of the pack. You then place the bottom portion on the top of the pack—thus placing the bridged card at the top of the pack.*) Proceed now directly to paragraph 4.

3. You should at this point create the impression that the cards are being indiscriminately mixed using a version of what is known as "Magician's Choice". (*For an explanation of this term see the relevant section of the chapter "Handling and Sleights-of-Hand.*") The outcome you want to achieve is to place Pile 4 and

Pile 1 together in any order (ie, 4 on 1, or 1 on 4), and Pile 3 and 2 together, again in any order. The two packets can then be placed together in any order (ie, 3—2—4—1, or 2—3—4—1, or 1—4—3—2, or 4—1—2—3). To do this proceed as follows: invite the spectator to choose any two of the four piles and to hand one to you. The spectator then places his or her pile face-down in front of him- or herself and you do the same with your pile in front of yourself. You then invite the spectator to choose any one of the other two piles and to hand the pile he or she has not selected to you. These piles are then placed by the sides of the previous piles. Having noted the positioning of the piles you now invite the spectator to select any one of his or her piles and to place it on any other pile. Depending upon his or her selection it is then possible to ensure that the required combination is produced as follows:

a. If the spectator places Pile 1 on 4, or Pile 4 on 1, or Pile 2 on 3, or Pile 3 on 2, he or she may combine the other two piles in any order and place the combined pair on the top of or at the bottom of the other pair.

b. If the spectator chooses any two piles which results in Pile 2 or 3 being combined with either Pile 1 or 4 then, having noted the order of the combination, the performer should place the other two piles appropriately at the top and/or bottom of the spectator's combined pile

4. Now deal out the top 13 cards of the pack face-down onto the table into two piles, dealing a card to each

pile in turn, beginning by dealing the first card to the left.

5. Then deal out the next 13 cards into a face-down pile in front of the spectator and instruct him or her to take the pile and to deal the cards out onto the two piles you have created. Ensure that the spectator deals the first card to the left, ie onto the right-hand pile from your point of view.

6. When the spectator's deal has been completed you deal the next 13 cards in turn onto the two piles on the table, again dealing first to your left onto the left-hand pile.

7. You now complete the procedure by dealing out the final 13 cards into a face-down pile in front of the spectator and instruct him or her to repeat the dealing at paragraph 5 above, again ensuring he or she deals first to the left, ie onto the right-hand pile from your point of view.

8. Having done so, invite the spectator to take any one of the piles, to turn it face-up, and to deal the cards out onto the table. You take the other pile and, turning it face-up, deal out from the top of the pile cards face-up onto the table. The spectator will deal out the cards of two suits in a numerical order. You will deal out the cards in an identical configuration.

ADDITIONAL TRICKS

THE ROUTINE AS DESCRIBED lasts for approximately 15 minutes. However, on some occasions, the performer may wish to extend it and, for this reason, four additional tricks are described in this chapter.

The tricks are designed to build on the routine, taking advantage of the fact that if either of the two finishes for the routine given in the chapter "*Adaptations and Alternatives*" are performed the cards will be in a known order or configuration. Additionally, two of the tricks ("*All In Order*" and "*You Can Find It*") can be performed as stand-alone tricks.

"All In Order"

1. This trick can be performed straight from the sealed carton or following on from any trick which has resulted in the cards being separated and placed in numerical order. In the latter case the numerical order can be either Ace to King or King to Ace for each suit, ie Clubs and Diamonds could be Ace to King and Spades and Hearts could be King to Ace or Clubs could be Ace to King and all the other suits King to Ace. If the trick is performed straight from the sealed carton the order of cards within the suits will be for the "*Bicycle Rider Pack*" and W.H. Smith "*Standard*" packs Hearts and Clubs: Ace to King, and Diamonds and Spades: King to Ace; and for the Waddington "*No 1*" pack King to Ace for all the suits. A third possibility is to perform the trick as a stand-alone trick at any convenient time in a routine, in which case the suits would be openly separated and arranged. In doing so make a mental note of the face card of the suit chosen by the spectator, ie either King or Ace.

2. Begin with the four suits in separate face-up piles on the table. Each will have either an Ace or a King as its top face-up card. Invite the spectator to select any one of the suits. When he or she has done so turn all the piles face-down.

3. Now take each pile in turn and perform a Charlier Shuffle. With each pile, when you have completed the shuffle, turn over the pile and place it face-up on the table. (*For an explanation of how to perform*

the Charlier Shuffle see the relevant section of the chapter "Handling and Sleights-of-Hand".) Having done this, ask the spectator to confirm his or her selected suit. Once the selection has been confirmed take whichever pile is the selected pile and turn it face-down. In doing so make a mental note of the top face-up card of the pile.

4.   Next ask the spectator to select any one of the other three piles. Once this is done, take the chosen pile and place it face-up on top of the face-down pile. Then take the other two face-up piles and riffle shuffle them (face-up) into each other. Having done this, riffle shuffle this face-up packet into the packet containing the selected cards. (*Note: This packet of cards will have the 13 face-up cards as the top cards of the packet and 13 face-down cards as the bottom cards of the packet.*)

5.   You now have the pack with the 13 cards of the selected suit spread throughout approximately the bottom half of the otherwise face-up pack. You then cut the pack taking off *a little less* than the top half of the pack and riffle shuffle the two halves of the pack together. (This, of course, will spread the cards of the selected suit throughout the whole of the pack. However, because of the Charlier Shuffle at paragraph 3 above they will not be in numerical order.)

6.   To bring the trick to its conclusion you now need to put them in numerical order. To do this proceed as follows:

   a.   Spread the pack to show the face-down cards spread throughout the face-up pack.

b. In doing this assume that the first face-down card you see is 1 less or 1 more in value than the card you noted at paragraph 3 above—1 less if the face-card of the selected suit was an Ace, and 1 more if the face-card of the selected suit was a King. Continue to spread the cards, mentally counting off the face-down cards as you come to them, counting *down* to the Ace if the face-card of the selected suit was an Ace, and *up* to the King if the face-card of the selected suit was a King. Irrespective of where you began the count note the position of the Ace or the King. When you have finished the spread cut the pack at that card to take it to what will be the bottom of the pack.

c. Now go through the pack again this time extracting the face-down cards in turn as you come to them, and placing them face-down in a pile on the table. As you go through the pack discard the face-up cards into a face-up pile on the table.

d. Now take the face down pile, turn it face-up, and deal out the selected suit in order. (*Note: Depending upon the accuracy of your cut at paragraph 5 above the Ace will be either the first or last card in the sequence.*)

"Same Number, Same Card"

1. This trick is described in my book *"Old Wine In A New Bottle"*. However, as it is an ideal trick to follow on from the previous trick *"All In Order"* it is appropriate to repeat it here. It can also be used following any trick which results in a numerical sequence of "10" to Ace or where such a sequence can be easily and secretly produced.

2. If you are using this trick as a follow-on trick from the trick *"All In Order"* you will have on the table a suit in numerical order Ace to King or "2" through King to Ace. Pick up all the cards on the table and re-constitute them into a face-down pack, taking care to place the numerical sequence as the bottom cards of the face-down pack. Then cut the pack into two roughly equal packets and hand the top "half" to the spectator, instructing him or her to extract the picture or court cards from it. You do the same for your "half" of the pack, again ensuring that the numerical sequence "10" to Ace is positioned at the bottom of the packet when it is turned face-down. When both of you have extracted the court cards from your packets, take the packet from the spectator and place it on top of your own packet. Then instruct the spectator to cut and complete the pack. (*For an explanation of the term "cut and complete" see the "Introduction".*)

3. If you are performing the trick as a stand-alone trick where the necessary numerical sequence is not immediately available proceed as follows: shuffle the

pack and then cut the pack into two roughly equal "halves". Hand one "half" to the spectator, who should extract the court cards, place them aside, and shuffle the remaining cards. Meanwhile, you extract the court cards from your "half" of the pack, place them aside, and, in doing so, as far as you are able, create a "10" to Ace sequence in the other cards. In discarding the court cards place them in a random face-up / face-down order. Take the shuffled cards from the spectator and hand him or her the face-up / face-down court cards. Instruct the spectator to go through them to ensure that there are no non-court cards in them. This should provide sufficient distraction to allow you to complete your "10" to Ace sequence and place it at the bottom of the face-down pack. You then place the pack face-down on the table and instruct the spectator to cut and complete it.

4.   Now instruct the spectator to choose any one of the court cards, to place the chosen card face-up on the table, and to assign to it any value from 1 to 10. He or she should make a note of or remember this number.

5.   You then take the pack and count off from the top of it a number of cards equal to the value the spectator has assigned to the court card. As the cards are counted their order is not reversed, ie. each card is counted off beneath the preceding card. The packet that is counted off it turned face-up to reveal the face card of the packet and the packet is then placed face-up on the court card so that only the left-hand

index of the court card can be seen. You then use the value of the face card of the packet as the number of cards you next count off the top of the pack. This packet is placed on the preceding packet as described above and the process is continued through the pack until you reach the final card of the pack or until there are insufficient cards left in the pack to match the value of the face card of the packet.

6. The values of all the revealed cards and the value assigned to the initial face-up court card are now added together.

7. The spectator is instructed to note and remember this number and to note and remember the identity of the card arrived at.

8. Having arrived at this total, you collect up all the cards from left to right, sliding each card or packet beneath the subsequent card or packet, and then place the pack face-down on the table, or the cards you have collected up face-down on the face-down cards you have left over from the counting out.

9. Now repeat the process described in paragraphs 5-8 above, having forecast that you will arrive at the same total and the same final card, and having allowed the spectator to assign a different number from 1 to 10 to the court card, which you take from the top of the pack and place face-up on the table. You will arrive at the same total and the same final card.

10. Collect up the cards as before, place the court card face-up on the table, and instruct the spectator to assign yet another value from 1 to 10 to it. Then go through the counting out procedure again and once again arrive at the same total and the same final card.

"*The Next Turn*"

1. This is a quick trick that can be performed after any other trick that produces a suit in numerical sequence or when such a sequence can be secretly arranged.

2. To perform the trick take the sequence of 13 cards and invite the spectator to cut and complete the packet a number of times. Then take the packet and perform a Charlier Shuffle. *(For an explanation of "cut and complete" see the "Introduction" and for a description of how to perform the Charlier Shuffle see the chapter on "Handling and Sleights-of-Hand".)*

3. Next invite the spectator to shuffle the remaining cards of the pack.

4. Return now to the 13 cards used at paragraph 2 above and invite the spectator to take any one of them and to note its identity secretly. When he or she has done this instruct him or her to place his or her card at any position within the packet. This having been done, take the packet and give it a Charlier Shuffle, allowing the spectator to determine how many cards are transferred at each stage of the shuffle.

5. Now take the remaining cards of the pack, invite the spectator to cut them into two roughly equal piles, then to take the packet from paragraph 4 above and to cut that into two roughly equal piles. He or she may then reconstitute the pack in any way he or she wishes, placing the piles one upon another in

any order. When that has been done, take the pack and perform a Charlier Shuffle. Finally, invite the spectator to cut the pack into two roughly equal packets. Take the packets and riffle shuffle them into each other. Having done this repeat the cutting and the shuffling once more. (*For a description of how to perform the riffle shuffle see the relevant section in the chapter "Handling and Sleights-of-Hand".*)

6. You now tell the spectator that you are going to deal out the pack and that while you are doing so you don't want any indication whatsoever as to the identity of his or her selected card. You then take the face-down pack and begin to deal out the cards from the top face-up into a pile on the table, placing the cards as they are dealt in an irregular pattern, ie so that no card completely covers the preceding card. As you are dealing out the cards mentally note the sequence in which the cards of the suit of the selected card are appearing. At some point the sequence will be broken and the card breaking the sequence will be the selected card. (*Note: The sequence may be, for example, K—Q—A—2—3—4—5—6—J—7— 8—9—10 or K—7—8—9—10—J—Q—A—2— 3—4—5—6. In the first sequence "J" would be the selected card and in the second sequence "K" would be the selected card.*

7. Irrespective of if you have noted the appearances of the selected card continue dealing out the cards until you have only one card left from the face-down pack. State then that the next card you turn over will

be the card selected by the spectator. As you make this statement go through the cards on the table and turn face-down in front of the spectator the selected card.

"You Can Find It"

1. For its best effect this trick should be performed using a bridged card and sleights-of-hand. It can, however, be performed without the bridged card and sleights-of-hand and a description of how this is done is set out at paragraphs 10-14 below.

2. To perform the trick using the bridged card and sleights-of-hand begin by handing the face-down pack to the spectator and instructing him or her to give it a thorough shuffle. When he or she has done so, take the pack back, place it face-down on the table and invite the spectator to cut it into two roughly equal packets. When this has been done take the two packets and riffle shuffle them together.

3. Having performed the shuffle, turn the pack face-up and begin to spread it, commenting upon the mix of the cards. In performing the spread what you are going to do is to cull or move four cards of the same identity (say, the "2s") to what will be the top of the pack when it is turned face-down. (*For a definition of the term "to cull" see the "Introduction" and for a description of how to perform the cull see the relevant section of the chapter "Handling and Sleights-of-Hand".*) Once the "2s" are in position at the top of the face-down pack, cut the bridged card from within the pack to place it at the bottom of the pack. (*For an explanation of how to do this see the relevant section of the chapter "Handling and Sleights-of-Hand".*)

4. You now have a face-down pack with the four "2s" as its top cards and the bridged card as its bottom card. Deal out face-down onto the table the top four cards of the pack, pick them up, mix their order, and invite the spectator to choose any one of them. He or she should make a secret note of its identity. You place the other three cards aside—still face-down.

5. You now invite the spectator to return the selected card to the "middle" of the face-down pack, and then cut and complete the pack. You then cut the bridged card to the bottom of the pack to place the selected card as the top card of the pack. (*For a definition of the term "cut and complete" see the "Introduction" and for details of how to use the bridged card in this handling see the relevant section of the chapter "Handling and Sleights-of-Hand".*)

6. Now take the three face-down cards you set aside at paragraph 4 above and, as instructed by the spectator, place them individually on the top or at the bottom of the face-down pack. When this has been done, perform a Charlier Shuffle and, finally, after the Shuffle, cut the bridged card to the bottom of the pack. Immediately, cut the pack into two roughly equal packets and riffle shuffle the two packets together, ensuring that the top four cards of the pack remain as the top four cards of the pack. (*For descriptions of the Charlier Shuffle and how to control the riffle shuffle see the relevant sections of the chapter "Handling and Sleights-of-Hand".*)

7. Place the face-down pack on the table and instruct the spectator to cut off from the top of the pack

about half the cards. When he or she has done so place the bottom "half" of the pack face-down in front of the spectator, and the "half" that has been cut off face-down in front of yourself. Having done so, instruct the spectator to cut the packet in front of you into two roughly equal packets.

8. You now instruct the spectator to go through the packet in front of him or her and find the selected card. As you are giving this instruction you place what was the bottom of the packet in front of yourself across what was the top of the packet.

9. When the spectator has discovered that the selected card is not in his or her packet comment that he or she might have better luck by taking the cards he or she cut to in the other packet. Take the cards that are across the top of this packet and place them aside. Hand the bottom cards to the spectator and instruct him or her to deal the top card face-up onto the table. It will be of the same value as the selected card but not the correct suit. The spectator may or may not comment on this. In any case, get him or her to confirm it is not the selected card and to try again by dealing the next card face-up onto the table. This, again, will be the correct value of the card but, again, not the correct suit—as will be the next card he or she deals face-up from the pack. Finally, get him or her to deal face-up the fourth card which will be his or her selected card.

10. The crux of the trick is to produce an initial situation in which the spectator chooses one card from all four cards of the same value, eg. the "2s", or the "6s", or

the "9s", etc. For its maximum effect the spectator should not be aware that he or she is selecting from "four of a kind", but, if it is not possible to achieve this, the trick, although weakened in its outcome, can be performed by allowing the spectator to choose with the cards openly displayed. Thus you would begin the trick by instructing the spectator to extract from the pack any four cards of the same value. However, there are ways in which you could secretly produce the necessary four cards as the top cards of a face-down pack without using any sleights-of-hand.

(1) The trick could be performed using the pack without the picture or court cards. This would require these cards to be extracted at the beginning of the trick thus providing you with the opportunity and distraction to make the necessary arrangement. To do this begin by handing "half" the pack to the spectator and instructing him or her to extract the court cards and to place them aside. You take the other "half" and do the same, taking the opportunity to collect as many cards of one "four of a kind" as you are able to at the top of your packet, say the "2s". In discarding the court cards place them in a pile on the table, some face-up and some face-down. When both you and the spectator have gone through your packets, take the spectator's packet and place it at the bottom of your own packet. Then instruct him or her to sort out the court cards and check they are all there (there should be 12) while you check the

pack. As you check the pack, if it is necessary, complete your "four of a kind" block of cards at the top of the face-down pack and, while you are doing this, also make a mental note of the bottom card of the face-down pack.

(2) The trick could be used as a follow-on trick from the trick "*Same Number, Same Card*" for the performance of which the court cards have already been extracted from the pack—11 of the court cards have been discarded and one of them (of which you know the identity) is at the top of the reconstituted face-down pack, say a Queen. Spread the court cards out face-up on the table and take one (*not* a Queen) and insert it face-down into the middle of the pack. Pick up another card (again *not* a Queen) and insert that card somewhere into the pack. Next pick up a Queen and place that card face-down on top of the pack. Take another card (of which you take a mental note, say Jack of Spades) and place that card at the bottom of the pack. Next take another card (*not* a Queen) and insert it within the pack, then take a Queen and place it at the bottom of the pack. This will leave you with five court cards on the table—one of which will be a Queen. Insert the cards which are not the Queen into the pack and place the Queen at the bottom of the pack. Then perform a Charlier Shuffle after which you should allow the spectator to cut and complete the pack. (*For an explanation of the term "cut and complete" see the "Introduction" and for*

details on how to perform the Charlier Shuffle see the relevant section of the chapter "Handling and Sleights-of-Hand".) This having been done, turn the pack face-up and spread it to show the mix of the cards. In performing this spread move the cards from right to left using the fingers of the left hand to pull the cards one above the other. At some point you will uncover the Jack of Spades. Immediately, place your left thumb on top of the next block of five or so cards to prevent them spreading and continue the spread by pulling the cards above them to the right with the right thumb. You then cut the spread to place the "Jack of Spades" as the bottom card of what will be the face down pack. In doing so, you will have placed the four Queens as the top four cards of the face-down pack.

11. By whatever way you have achieved it you now have either "four of a kind" face-up cards on the table or "four of a kind" face-down cards as the top cards of the face-down pack. If the former then turn them face-down and mix them; if the latter deal the top four cards face-down onto the table and mix them.

12. Now invite the spectator to take any one of the four cards and to note it secretly. While he or she is doing this, you should secretly note the bottom card of the face-down pack, and place the other three cards aside.

13. You now invite the spectator to return the selected card to the top of the face-down pack. You then take the cards you placed aside at paragraph 12

above and place them individually at the top or at the bottom of the pack as directed by the spectator. Once this has been done, perform a Charlier Shuffle and then allow the spectator to cut and complete the pack. Finally, turn the pack face-up and spread it to show the mix of the cards. In doing this follow the procedure described at paragraph 10 above. (This will place the "four of a kind" as the top cards of the face-down pack with the selected card as the 4th card from the top of the pack.

14. Now proceed to bring the trick to its conclusion as described at paragraphs 7-9 above.

HANDLING AND
SLEIGHTS-OF-HAND

THIS CHAPTER DESCRIBES THE various techniques
that can be used to manipulate and control the cards. It
is, for the most part, reproduced from the companion
volumes "*Old Wine In A New Bottle*" and "*Magic Aces*".
However, some amendments to the handling have been
made and some additional material has been added (eg,
Culling A Card or Cards).

It is not intended that the newcomer to card magic
should work methodically through the material studying
and practising each technique. Such a procedure would
not only be counter-productive but also boring in the
extreme. Rather what is intended is that the reader
should use the chapter as a reference source on the
various techniques, turning to it as required during the
study of the various tricks, and, for this reason, extensive
references are made to this chapter in the descriptions of
the performance of the tricks. However, the beginner is
strongly advised to master at the very outset a number of
essential skills. These are:

The Overhand Shuffle
The Riffle Shuffle
A False Cut
A False Shuffle

With regard to the use of the techniques a word of warning is appropriate: **do not over-use them**. They do allow you to create the illusion of the cards being indiscriminately mixed. They do allow you to place cards in positions in a pack or packet that facilitate an effect. However, if they are used when they are not essential (either as a habit or to give you a degree of personal satisfaction in deluding the audience) their very use will give rise to suspicion and the spectators, seeing the moves used so often, will begin to look carefully at them and thus might detect the subterfuge involved.

Practise the techniques to the point at which they are almost automatic in performance and do not look at your hands when performing them. If you look at your hands the chances are that the spectators will too and what would go unobserved will be closely examined.

The Overhand Shuffle

Hold the pack, face-down, with the outer end towards the spectators. The cards' outer sides should rest on the part of the palm at the junction between the palm and the fingers at an angle of about 45°, the inner side upward. The thumb rests across the top card of the pack, and the first finger is against the outer corner. The other fingers rest on the face of the bottom card.

Using the hand not holding the pack lift up the bottom half or so of the pack with the thumb holding the inner end of the packet and the first three fingers at the outer end.

Move the packet over the top of the other packet and pull off from the top of it single cards or clumps of cards with the thumb of the hand holding what was the top part of the pack, allowing the cards or single card to fall onto that packet as the packet in the other hand is moved backwards and forwards.

Carry on with this procedure until all the cards have been pulled off what was the bottom of the pack onto what was the top of the pack.

To continue the shuffle, again cut away the bottom half or so of the pack and go through the procedure again.

Controlling the Cards

The top card can be taken to the bottom of the pack by slipping the card off the top of the pack as the shuffle begins and immediately shuffling off the rest of the pack onto it, ie. the whole pack other than the top card is lifted to begin the shuffle.

The bottom card of the pack can be moved to the top of the pack by beginning the shuffle by lifting about the bottom $2/3$ of the pack. This packet is held between the thumb at the inner end and the second and third fingers at the outer end. As the shuffle progresses pressure is exerted on the final card in the packet to ensure that it is the final card shuffled off.

To hold the bottom card at the bottom of the pack the shuffle begins by lifting the packet which will be shuffled off from the middle of the pack and allowing the top and bottom remaining packets to fall together.

To transpose the top and bottom cards of the pack begin by slipping the top card as described above for taking the top card to the bottom. Then shuffle off all the other cards onto it exerting pressure on the final card (what was the bottom card of the pack) to ensure that this card is the final card shuffled off.

The Riffle Shuffle

Hold the pack face-down with the outer side of the pack towards the spectators. The pack is held with both hands, the thumbs at the inner side and the fingers at the outer side.

Split the pack into two halves, moving the top half to the left and the bottom half to the right, and place the two halves face-down on the table end to end, the outer sides of the packets still towards the spectators.

Move the two packets against each other until the two inner corners are touching and form the point a V with the open end of the V facing the spectators.

Change the position of the hands holding the packets so that the thumbs are immediately behind the corners forming the point of the V, the little fingers at the corners of the outside ends, the first fingers pressing down on the packets at the open part of the V. The little fingers are pushing at the end outside corners. The other fingers are at the outer sides of the packets.

Push down with all the fingers and at the same time lift the inner sides off the table with the thumbs, keeping the two corners forming the sharp end of the V in close contact.

Allow the cards to fall away in a cascade from the bottom of each packet interleaving with each other as they fall.

Close the V by pushing the inner ends of the two packets together thus completely inter-weaving them.

Push the two packets into each other and square up the pack.

Controlling the Cards

To retain the top card or a top block of cards at the top of the shuffled pack control the release of the left hand packet (ie. what was the top half of the pack) so that the desired card or cards drop last.

To retain the bottom card or a bottom block of cards at the bottom of the shuffled pack allow the bottom card or the bottom cards of the right hand packet (ie. what was the bottom half of the pack) to fall first.

The Charlier Shuffle

With the outer ends of the cards facing the spectators, the pack is placed face-down diagonally across the up-turned palm immediately adjoining the base of the fingers. The thumb is at the outer side of the pack towards the outer corner and the tips of the fingers curl around the inner side.

The basic shuffle (or, rather, mix) begins by the other hand (palm down) moving over the pack. The thumb of this hand is at the inner end of the pack with the top of the third finger curling over the outer end towards the inner corner. The pack is then tilted, the outer side of the pack pivoting on the upturned palm of the up-turned hand.

The upper hand now slides out a small packet of cards from the **bottom** of the pack, leaving the remainder of the pack resting on the fingers of the lower hand, the thumb of which moves onto the top of the pack.

This thumb now pushes off a small packet of cards from the **top** of what was the pack and these cards are slid **beneath** the cards held in the other (down-turned) hand.

The fingers of the up-turned hand now push off a small packet of cards from the **bottom** of what was the pack and these cards are placed on the **top** of the cards in the other (down-turned) hand.

This alternating top and bottom extraction of cards is continued until all the cards that constituted the original pack have been transferred and the shuffle (or mix) is complete. The rule to be remembered is that cards taken from the bottom go on top, and cards taken from the top go to the bottom.

Controlling the Cards

Although the cards appear to have been thoroughly mixed the outcome of the shuffle is the same as would have resulted if the pack had been cut and completed. So, if at the end of the shuffle you cut the original bottom card of the pack back to the bottom of the pack then the pack will be back in its original order. Alternatively, if you had started with a bridged card at the bottom of the pack and if you cut it back to the bottom of the pack after the shuffle you would restore the pack to its original order.

Another method of controlling the mix when using a small packet of cards is to note the number of cards being transferred during the mix and then to perform a second mix transferring the same sequence of cards but this time starting the mix from the top of the pack. For example, if on the first mix of a 12-card packet you take four cards off the bottom, three off the top, two off the bottom, leaving three cards to be placed at the bottom and you then on the second mix take four cards off the top, three of the bottom, two off the top, leaving three cards to be placed on the top, the pack will be back in its original order. It might be thought that such handling would be immediately noted by the spectators but if it is done boldly and quickly it will be accepted as a fair mix of the pack.

Creating and Handling a Bridged Card

There are a number of ways in which the bottom card of the pack may be handled to produce a convex bridge.

For the first, hold the pack face down with the outer end towards the spectators. The thumb is positioned on the outer side and the fingers wrap around the inner side. Move the other hand over the pack, the thumb at the inner end of the pack and the fingers at the outer end, and lift the pack very slightly, allowing the bottom card to fall onto and rest on the palm of the hand originally holding the pack, the separation of the card being facilitated by a slight upward pressure by the thumb of the upper hand on the rest of the pack, and the procedure being concealed by tilting the pack, ie. raising the inner end. Squeeze the card at its sides using the fingers of the lower hand to press the card against the fleshy part of the palm at the base of the thumb of the same hand. Only very slight pressure to produce a very slight bridge is required. Then allow the pack to drop back onto the card. The bottom card is bridged along its length with a convex bridge.

For the second, again hold the pack face-down with the outer end towards the spectators. The pack rests on the palm of the hand with the thumb at the outer side and the fingers wrapped around the inner side. The other hand moves over the pack and lifts it leaving the bottom card in the palm of the hand originally holding the pack.

The pack is then turned so that the inner side points downwards towards the single card. The cards are then allowed to fall in a cascade onto the single card which is held between the fingers and thumbs of the lower hand. This will produce a "round of applause" (ie. the sound of cards falling onto the single card). More significantly, it produces a convex bridge of the card along its length.

A third method, which again allows you to bridge the card quite openly without raising any suspicion in the spectators, is to play with the pack in a very casual way while you are chatting with them. In doing so order the cards so that the card you wish to bridge is either the top card or bottom card of the face-down pack. When this has been achieved suddenly cut the pack into two roughly equal packets and hand the packet not containing the card you wish to bridge to a spectator, instructing him or her to shuffle it. While he or she is doing so you shuffle the packet you have retained to either take the top card to the bottom or the bottom card to the top and then back to the bottom, depending upon the initial position of the card you wish to bridge. At this point the spectator is likely to have completed his or her shuffle. Ask him or her to either give the packet another good shuffle or, if there is more than one spectator, to pass it to another spectator for them to shuffle. As this is being done turn your packet face-up and, while playing with the cards as you watch and chat with the spectator/s, take the top face-up card and, under cover of the hand not holding the packet, give that card a convex bridge along its length. Once you have done this cut the packet to place the bridged card roughly in the middle of the packet and turn the packet face-down. Now exchange packets with the spectator/s, instructing them to shuffle the second packet while you shuffle the other packet. The two packets are then placed together to reconstitute the pack (with somewhere within it your bridged card).

For some occasions (eg. for pre-prepared (or "stacked") tricks of a routine) you are able to produce the bridged card prior to the performance in which you are going to use it. In which case, if the pre-prepared trick you are going to use it for allows it, once you have created the bridged card cut it into the middle of the pack before placing the pack in its carton.

You should note that only a very slight bridge is required to produce the desired outcome and that during performance (particularly after riffle shuffles) it may be necessary to "refresh" the bridge.

Handling a Bridged Card

To cut the bridged card from within the pack hold the pack loosely, the outer end towards the spectators, with the face of the cards facing outwards and the backs inwards. The thumb is very loosely on the top side of the pack and the fingers are gently supporting the bottom side from beneath. The other hand (again very gently) rests on the pack, the thumb at the inside end and the fingers at the outer end. The pressure of the thumb on the top side of the pack is relaxed, and the pack is allowed to open at the natural break. The bottom section of the pack will fall into the palm of the hand. You lift away this bottom packet of the pack and place it face-down on top of the pack. This should put the bridged card to the bottom of the re-constituted pack. It is prudent, however, to check that this has been achieved and this can be done by glimpsing the card at the bottom of the pack. To do this, after you have completed the cut, turn the face-down pack so that the back of the cards are towards the spectators with the sides of the cards at top and bottom. Hold the pack with both hands, the back of the hands towards the spectators and with the thumbs on the face of the pack and the fingers on the back of the pack. Tap the bottom side of the pack on the table to square up the cards and, in doing so, glimpse the identity of the bottom card. Once you have done so turn the pack face-down and place it on the table. If you do not glimpse the required card have the pack cut again or cut the pack yourself and repeat the whole procedure.

To allow the pack to be cut and to then restore it to its original order begin with the bridged card at the bottom of the face-down pack and allow the pack to be cut and completed. Then cut the bridged card to the bottom of the pack as described in the previous paragraph. To control a selected card which has been returned to either the top or the bottom of the pack after the pack has been cut and completed begin with the bridged card either at the top or at the bottom of the pack and allow a spectator to replace his or her selected card on the top or at the bottom of the pack. Then allow the spectator to cut and complete the pack as many times as he or she wishes. If you then cut the bridged card to the bottom of the pack the selected card will be the top card of the pack.

To control a selected card returned to the "the middle of the pack" after the pack has been cut and completed begin with the bridged card at the bottom of the pack.

Cut off the top half of the face-down pack and place it face-down on the table in front of the spectator. He or she places the selected card on top of this packet and you place what was the bottom half of the pack on top of the selected card. The spectator may now cut and complete, at will. Finally, you cut the bridged card to the bottom of the pack, which places the selected card at the top of the pack. Alternatively, with the pack in hand, cut off the top half of the pack with the other hand and hold this packet face-down towards the spectator for him or her to place the selected card on top of it. Then place what was the bottom of the pack face-down on top of the spectator's card. You then proceed as described above, allowing the spectator to cut and complete before you finally cut the bridged card to the bottom of the pack.

To disguise the use of a bridged card or to retain a card or block of cards at the top of the pack, having cut the bridged card to the bottom of the pack begin the procedure again. This time, in relaxing the pressure of the thumb on the top side of the pack, allow approximately the bottom 1/3 of the pack to fall away into the palm. Now using the index finger of the other hand you open the top 2/3 of the pack as if opening a book and insert what was the bottom 1/3 of the pack into the gap thus formed and then close the pack. The bridged card is now approximately 2/3 of the way down the pack. Repeat this procedure allowing the cards **below** the bridged card to fall into the palm of your hand. As you did before open up a gap in the other cards and place the cards from your palm in it. When the pack is closed the bridged card will be at the bottom of the pack.

False Cuts

If you are using a bridged card the illusion of a fair cut is easily achieved (beginning with the bridged card at the bottom of the pack) by casually cutting and completing the pack two or more times before cutting the bridged card to the bottom of the pack. If, however, you are not using a bridged card or if the bridged card is and must remain within the pack then the illusion must be achieved by other means. One straight-forward (but still deceptive) procedure is to begin with the pack face-down with the outer side towards the spectators. The pack is held with both hands, the thumbs at the inner side and the fingers at the outer side. Tilt the pack, raising the inner side with the thumbs, and then with the right hand pull the bottom $1/3$ of the pack to the right and place it face down on the top of the pack, out-jogged on the outer end of the pack by about half an inch. The consequent out-jog at the inner end of the pack is concealed by the back of the left hand. Repeat the movement for the next $1/3$ of the pack from the bottom of the pack—this time placing the cut-off packet directly on top of the out-jogged packet. Now push down with the left little finger on what is the concealed out-jogged bottom $1/3$ of the packet and pull that packet to the right under the pack with the right hand, placing it on the top of the pack. The pack is then in its original order. The procedure when performed quickly and slickly gives the illusion of a genuine cut.

False Shuffles

The simplest false shuffle is what is normally described as the "optical shuffle". If it is performed confidently and smoothly, without looking at the hands or attracting the attention of the spectators to the hands, it is a very deceptive false shuffle. To perform it begin with the pack in position for an overhand shuffle as described earlier in this chapter. Cut away about the bottom ²/3 of the pack and, as in the genuine overhand shuffle, move this packet over the top of the other packet. Do so until it completely covers the other packet without relaxing your grip of it. As the cut-away packet moves over the packet that was the top of the pack place the thumb of the hand holding this packet on top of the cut-off packet, then take the bottom ²/3 you cut-off upwards, as you do so allowing the thumb to slip along the top card of the upward moving packet **but do not release any cards from the packet**. Once the packet has cleared what was the bottom ¹/3 of the pack move it down behind that packet and allow a small block of cards to fall onto the bottom of that packet. Continue the procedure until all the cards from what was the bottom part of the pack have been placed behind what was the top ¹/3 of the pack. The illusion of a true shuffle can be heightened by, when the ²/3 packet is moved behind the ¹/3 packet, the cards of the ¹/3 packet are allowed to tilt towards the thumb of the hand holding them.

Another straight-forward and effective false shuffle again begins with the cards in the position for an overhand shuffle. Take about the bottom ¾ of the pack and lift it above the other cards as if beginning a standard overhand shuffle. At the same time the thumb of the lower hand pulls the top ¼ of the pack down onto the fingers of that hand and moves this packet under what was the bottom ¾ of the pack. A break or gap is held between what was the upper ¼ of the pack and what was the bottom ¾ of the pack using the thumb and fingers of the hand holding the pack. Continue pulling of small blocks of cards from the top of what was the bottom ¾ of the pack, placing these blocks beneath what was the top ¼ of the pack, maintaining the gap or break. When all the cards have been transferred the pack will be back in its original order. The secret of success with this false shuffle (which is, in fact, a series of cuts off the top of the pack being transferred to the bottom of the pack in order) is to keep the gap or break as small as possible and to hide it with what was the bottom ¾ of the pack by tilting the pack towards the spectators. The illusion created is of the cards being shuffled into the bottom part of the pack.

A False Mix

The impression can be given that a pack or block of cards is being thoroughly mixed when, in fact, no change is being made in its order. To do this begin with a bridged card at the bottom of the pack or packet and by then performing a Charlier Shuffle as described earlier in this chapter. You may, if you wish, during the shuffle allow a spectator to determine how many cards you take from the top and from the bottom of the pack or packet. Having completed the shuffle you place the pack face-down on the table, cut off the top ¾ of the pack, and place this packet by the side of what was the bottom of the pack (A). Now cut off the top ¾ of the packet you took off A and place these cards by the side of what was this packet (B). Now cut off the top half of the packet you have placed beside B and place it by the side of what was the bottom of this packet (C). The last packet is D. You now have on the table four packets D—C—B—A. Place A on D and B on AD and then invite a spectator to determine whether C is placed on top of or beneath BAD. Do as he or she wishes and then perform a second Charlier Shuffle. Both you and the spectators may now cut and complete, at will. Finally, you cut the bridged card to the bottom of the pack and the pack is then back in its original order.

Culling A Card Or Cards

The ability to cull or extract a card secretly from within the pack to move it to a more advantageous position (usually the top of the face-down pack) opens up many opportunities for the performer of card magic.

The handling by which such a cull is achieved begins by turning the pack face-up with the outer end towards the spectators, the pack tilting slightly downward towards them. The pack is held with both hands (palms up)—the fingers beneath the cards and the thumbs on the face of the cards.

Ostensibly to show the mix of the cards, you then begin to spread the pack, pushing the cards either right to left with the right thumb or left to right with the left thumb, each card as it is pushed along moving beneath the preceding card. The spread as it progresses rests on the fingers of the receiving hand. When you see the card you wish to place at the top of the face-down pack the first or index finger of the receiving hand moves onto the face of that card as it is pushed along (ie, the nail of the finger makes contact above the advancing side of the card). This places the fingers of the receiving hand at the back of the selected card and, while the spread continues, the card is drawn towards the outside edge of the receiving packet. Simultaneously, the packet from which the cards are being pushed is moved very slightly upwards, sufficient only to allow the tips of the fingers of the pushing hand to open up a small gap between the selected card and the receiving packet. Once this has been done the cards as they are pushed across the spread will move over the selected card—and the first finger of the receiving hand can move back to its position below the selected card. The spread can then be cut at any subsequent point, which will place the selected card at the top of the pack when the pack is turned face-down, or the whole pack can be spread producing the same result.

To cull a number of cards from within the pack to the top of the pack begin as you would in culling a single card as described above. Once the first card you wish to cull is in position beneath the cards in the receiving hand and the subsequent cards of the spread are being pushed above it, insert the tip of the fingers of the pushing hand above the first selected card. This will ensure that the small gap between the selected card and the receiving packet is maintained and allow the fingers of the receiving hand to fix the selected card in position beneath the spread. When you come to the next card you wish to cull withdraw the tips of the fingers from the gap. At the same time, using the thumb of the pushing hand, fix one or two cards preceding it in the spread, and, using the fingers of the remaining hand, pull the selected card underneath them and to the outside edges of the receiving packet. In doing this the selected card will move beneath the previously selected card and will move clear of the cards that have been fixed by the pushing thumb. As the spread is continued the cards that were fixed will move above the first selected card and the fingers of the pulling hand are able to restore that gap above it. The process continues in this way until all the required cards are in position.

Using A Key Card

A key card is used to allow the performer to locate and, if necessary, to manipulate the position of an unknown card placed in the pack by a spectator. If it is used to locate and identify the unknown card the performer ensures that when the unknown card is placed in the pack the key card (of which the performer knows the identity) is placed next to it or in a known proximity to it. The manipulations required to allow this to be done are the same as are described for handling a bridged card when a selected card is placed in "the middle of the pack" and when the key card is the original bottom card of the face-down pack. What is then required to identify the unknown card is for the performer to spread the cards face-up to show the mix of the cards and to identify the unknown card by its position in relation to the key card. The manipulation to move the now identified card to a position advantageous for the performer is again achieved as with a bridged card, ie. the pack is cut so that the key card will be the bottom card of the pack when the pack is turned face-down. This will place the selected card as the top card of the face-down pack.

The essential skill required by the performer is the ability to spread and cut the pack when it is face-up without arousing any suspicion in the spectator. If the cards are spread from right to left with the thumb of the right hand, pushing each card under the preceding card, then the selected card will be immediately above the key card and must be quickly pulled out of view under the preceding cards. If the cards are spread from right to left, sliding the cards with the fingers of the left hand from the bottom of the pack with each card moving above the preceding card, then the key card will be located first and the selected card can be hidden by suppressing it in the spread. In this case, of course, the performer will not be able to identify the selected card. He or she will, however, be able to position it as the top card of the face-down pack.

Magician's Choice

Magician's Choice (or, as it is sometimes referred to by the French word meaning ambiguous—"equivoque") is a means of producing the outcome in a spectator's choice of card or cards that is required by the performer. Its success depends upon the way in which the choice is presented to the spectator and the way in which the response is interpreted by the performer.

An example of a multiple choice illustrates the principle involved.

You begin by placing five cards or five packets of cards on the table—say A, B, C, D, and E, with A being the required card or packet. The spectator is asked to "pick out" any four cards or packets and to touch the cards or packets. If the spectator chooses B, C, D, and E you pick up those cards or packets and place them aside, leaving you with the required card or packet. If the spectator chooses A and three other cards or packets discard the card or packet he has not chosen and proceed to another choice. You now have on the table A and, say, B, C, and D, and you ask the spectator "now to choose any two of the four that are left". If the spectator chooses any two of B, C, or D discard those cards or packets, leaving A and one other card or packet. If the spectator chooses A and another card or packet, discard the other two cards or packets, again leaving A and one other card or packet. You now have A and one other card or packet on the table and you now ask the spectator "to pick out one of those cards / packets". If he or she chooses A then you discard the other card or packet. If he or she chooses the other card or packet you discard that. In any case, you finish with the required card on the table.

SOURCES AND BACKGROUND

THIS CHAPTER GIVES THE background against which the effects and the handling of the tricks were developed. It also, where appropriate, adds a little information to the descriptions of the handling and sleights-of-hand in the previous chapter.

Arranging And Setting The Pack

It has already been noted that when the "*Bicycle Rider Back*" pack is removed from its carton, and the Jokers and extraneous cards removed, it is in the order Ace to King (Hearts), Ace to King (Clubs), King to Ace (Diamonds), King to Ace (Spades). Such an arrangement is known as a "*Rusduck Stay Stack*", so called from the name of the card performer, John Russell Duck, who developed a variety of effects using it. What he noted was that if a pack of cards so arranged was cut into two equal packets and the two packets were perfectly inter-weaved either one or more times then the halves of the packs are always mirror images of each other in relation to the values and positioning of the cards. It follows therefore that if the original order of the pack is changed to Ace to King (Clubs), Ace to King (Hearts), King to Ace (Diamonds), King to Ace (Spades) then the outcome of this interweaving will be that the halves of the pack will be mirror images of each other in relation not only to the value and positioning of the cards but also in relation to the colour of the cards, ie, the Black "2s", the Red "9s" will match, etc. The arrangement of the pack as described in the relevant section of the chapter "*The Routine*" organises the pack into the appropriate configuration to produce this outcome.

Ideally, the pack should then be set by what are known as "*faro*" shuffles, where the cards are divided into two equal packets and then perfectly inter-weaved into each other. The technique required to produce such a result is difficult and, except in the hands of a very experienced and adept performer, unreliable. There are, however, other means by which the same outcome may be produced. One is by dealing out the cards into two packets followed by placing one packet on the other. Another is by using what Jean Tamariz in his book "*Mnemonica*" terms the "*anti-faro*", which entails dealing out the cards into four piles followed by a pick-up in reverse order to the order of the dealing. A second such deal will distribute the colours more thoroughly while still maintaining a mirror image order. A third will arrange the pack in matching pairs in the sequence: Aces, Kings, "2s", Queens, "3s, Jacks, "4s", "10s", "5s", "9s", "6s", "8s", "7s". A fourth deal would restore the pack to its original order.

For the reader who wishes to attempt to master the faro shuffle it can be performed either on the table or in the hands off the table. For the former begin by splitting the pack into two equal packets and placing them inner end to inner end. In holding the packets the thumbs should be at about the middle of the back sides of the packets, the index fingers should rest on the top of the packets, the second and third fingers should be on the front sides of the packets at the outer corners, and the little fingers should be at the outer ends of the packets at the front corners. Raise the inner touching ends of the packets by pushing the two packets together and thus forming a convex bend in each packet. In performing this move ensure that the tips of the second, third and little fingers and the thumbs maintain contact with the table. Once the convex bend has been produced in the packets weave the two packets into each other by moving the packets against each other front to back and back to front. Do not force the cards into each other—rather allow the tension created by the bend in the packets to inter-weave the cards.

To perform the shuffle in the hands and off the table begin again with the two packets end to end. One packet is held with the hand palm down and the other with the palm up. The thumbs of each hand are at the middle of the back sides of the packets. The first three fingers of the palm-down hand are at the front sides of the packets and the little finger abuts against the middle of the outside edge. With the palm-up hand the second and third fingers are at the front side of the cards at the middle of the packet, the index finger is at the middle of the outside end, and the little finger is lightly touching the bottom of the packet. The two packets are then pushed together to produce a convex bend in each packet with tension between the two packets. Then using this tension allow the two packets to inter-weave. In doing so do not attempt to force the cards.

In both procedures some performers prefer to angle the packets so that the two inner corners at the back of the pack only are in contact. Then, the weave having been made at that point, the packets are brought together to allow the cards to be pushed together.

"Cards And Numbers"

As the cards are configured so that the two halves of the pack are mirror images of each other the requirement for the performer is to know the position of the card selected in the spectator's half in order to calculate the position of the matching card in his or her own packet. In the second part of the trick this is achieved by what is usually referred to as "The Principle of 9", which is a method of producing the number 9 from any number from 10 to 19. The "principle" is that for any such number if the two digits of the number are added together to give a single digit number and if that number is then subtracted from the original two digit number the result will always be 9, eg:

$$(10 = 1 + 0 = 1) \qquad (10 - 1 = 9)$$
$$(17 = 1 + 7 = 8) \qquad (17 - 8 = 9)$$
$$(19 = 1 + 9 = 10) \qquad (19 - 10 = 9)$$

Because the routine as a whole requires that the order of the cards within the pack is preserved the handling for this trick ensures that the selected card will always be what is the 10th card down in the spectator's half of the face-down pack.

For those readers who would like to study further the potential of this and some other numerical principles when applied to card magic the book "*Card Concepts*" by Arthur F. MacTier is recommended, as is Martin Gardner's "*Mathematics, Magic, and Mystery*".

"*Bluff—Double Bluff*"

The reader will have noted from the comments on the setting of the pack given earlier in this chapter that a third dealing out of the cards (equivalent to a third faro shuffle) from a Rusduck Stay Stack not only produces the two halves of the pack in mirror images but also produces mirror images of the cards by pairs. This trick, "*Bluff—Double Bluff*", takes advantages of this arrangement, which has been arrived at by the second dealing out in the previous trick "*Cards And Numbers*". All that is then required to arrange the cards for the successful outcome of "*Bluff—Double Bluff*" is to reverse the order of the spectator's half of the pack.

Separating The Cards

The outcome of this trick derives from an observation by Norman Gilbreath that if a pack of cards, where the cards are distributed throughout the pack in alternating colours, is cut so that the bottom cards of the two packets are of different colours, then, if the two packets are riffle shuffled together and the cards dealt out in pairs, each pair will contain a card of each colour. The order in which the colours occur cannot be predicted, but there will always be one card of each colour.

For a full discussion of the principles arising from this observation and the variety of uses to which they may be put in card magic the reader is referred to Arthur F. MacTier's book "*Card Concepts*".

"*All In Order*"

This trick combines the principal feature of the Charlier Shuffle with that of the riffle shuffle.

The Charlier Shuffle (named after the French card performer who developed it) ensures that the cards, although apparently randomly mixed, remain in the order that would have resulted had the cards been merely cut and completed. Thus the cards can be restored to their original order by handling that returns what was the bottom card back to that position. The reader might be interested to note that Jean Hugard in his book "*The Royal Road To Card Magic*" observed that of all the false shuffles that there are "for… laymen (the Charlier Shuffle) is the most convincing false shuffle extant," and the beginner in card magic might be pleased to know that he also observes that the shuffle is "most effective when done rather clumsily".

The riffle shuffle ensures that when two packets of cards are riffle shuffled together, although the packets are mixed together, the original order of each packet remains the same. Readers who would be interested to see the various effects that can be produced using the shuffle should see the chapter "*Riffle-Shuffle Setups*" in Karl Fulves' book "*More Self-Working Card Tricks*".

"*Same Number—Same Card*"

In his book *Card Concepts* Arthur F. MacTier sets out and discusses two "principles" involving counting sequences using packs of cards. The first was developed by Martin D. Kruskel and the second came from an effect developed by Alexander F. Kraus. The former is based on the fact that if you take a pack of cards and turn over the first card at the top of the pack and then go to the card at the position in the pack indicated by the value of the first card and turn that card over, take the value of that card as a new starting point and go through the pack repeating this process, you will eventually arrive at the last card in the pack or at a card with a value greater than the number of the cards left in the pack. If this card is noted and the whole process is repeated, again and again, using the second card of the pack as the starting point, then the third, then the fourth, etc. there is a fair probability that you will finish the sequence on the same card. In fact, the probability is the probability of the sequencing coinciding at some point. This probability can be significantly increased by a number of subterfuges, eg. by counting the picture or court cards as 10s, or, even better, as 1s. MacTier then describes a very elegant and striking effect using this principle. It uses two packs of cards. In essence the trick consists of the spectator and the performer each thinking of a number from 1 to 10 and using that number as the starting point of the process described above for their own pack. The packs are then exchanged, the order of the packs not being disturbed. The spectator and the performer then go through the counting process again, this time using their own thought-of number as the starting point. Each should arrive at the other's card. Although the probability of success is quite high it is still only a probability, and MacTier considers it prudent to provide a means of disguising failure. However, the second principle can have a guaranteed outcome in that if a sequence of cards from King through to Ace is placed on the bottom of a pack and if a card is taken from near the top of the pack and used as the first card in the counting process then the total of the turned-up cards will always be 52. Moreover, the cards above the stack may be shuffled on each count and there is no requirement to adjust the values of the high value cards thus they can be given their actual values: "J" (11), "Q" (12), "K" (13). It occurred to me that the two "principles" could be combined to use the guaranteed outcome of the second "principle" to disguise the fact that the first "principle" had not led to a successful outcome. In fact, given that the totalling effect

would work every time, there was a fair probability that
the "each participant finds the other's card" would work
and a very fair probability that one of the cards would be
arrived at in the counting-out process. However, there are
further variations of the second "principle" from which
it is possible to develop other effects with a guaranteed
outcome. The first variation I tried was of retaining the
King to Ace stack at the bottom of the pack and cutting
a number of cards from the top of the pack. Thus, when
you have completed the counting out process described
above the number of cards cut off would be equal to 52
minus the total arrived at by the counting process. For
example, if you could secretly remove say five cards from
the pack before the counting out began then you could
predict that the total arrived at would be 47 (52 - 5).
Alternatively, you could allow a spectator to select the
starting point in the pack for the count (say, the 5th card
down) and predict that the total arrived at would be 48
(52 - 5 = 47 + 1 = 48). If the selected starting point was
the 15th card in the pack then the total arrived at would
be 38 (52 - 15 = 37 plus 1 = 38). The second variation I
tried was to place a King through Ace stack at the top of
the pack and a King through Ace stack at the bottom of
the pack. With this pre-arrangement it would be possible
to predict that the total arrived at by the counting process
would be 52 minus the selected number plus 1. You
could also, if the count was repeated without disturbing
the order of the pack, but with a different starting point,
predict that the total arrived at would be 52 minus the
second selected number plus 1, and that at the end of the
second count you would arrive at the same card as on the
first count. In fact, the second card in the counting process

will always begin the same sequence irrespective of what number is selected as the starting point, ie. it will be the 14th card from the top of the pack. The third variation of this second "principle" arises from the observation that it can be applied to a packet of cards as well as to the whole pack. For example, if you remove from the pack the picture or count cards you will be left with a packet of 40 cards. If you then place a "10" through to Ace at the bottom of this packet and ask a spectator at what number card in the packet he or she wishes to begin the counting process, the total that will be arrived at will be 40 minus the number selected plus 1. If you repeat the process for another number, without disturbing the order of the packet, you will arrive at a different total number but one that you could have predicted immediately the spectator had chosen at what point in the packet he or she wished the counting process to start. All these variations had the potential to produce a strong effect but obviously there were many more variations hidden away behind the principle which had equal potential. I determined to try to find some of the them. After much experimentation I came to a number of conclusions. The first was that the stack at the top of the pack could be eliminated either by using a thought-of number or by using a card to which the spectator could assign any value. My second conclusion was that in the counting processes leading to an over-all total I could allow the spectator to choose any card in the packets counted out without affecting the eventual outcome of the total number: it was only when I wished to arrive at the same card in two counts that the cards needed to be kept in the same order within the packets. The third conclusion arose out of the need to disguise the placing of the stack at the bottom of the pack and I concluded that this could be achieved by misdirecting the attention of the spectator by asking him or her to sort though the cards in the pack extracting certain cards and that the most logical cards for the spectator to be searching for were the picture or court cards. This line of thought re-inforced my next conclusion that a number of cards less than the full pack produced a less suspicion-inducing total than the 52 produced by the full pack. It also reduced the stack from thirteen down to a more manageable ten cards. However, my most startling conclusion was that if the "10" to Ace sequence was placed *within* the pack then not only did it guarantee that the dealing would finish on the same card but it also guaranteed that the total arrived at would (if the order of the cards was not disturbed) always be the same irrespective of the starting number. A few moments thought shows why. After entry into the "10" to Ace sequence the subsequent cards will always be the same and thus have the same total number. The cards preceeding the "10" to Ace sequence plus the card arrived at in the sequence will also have the same total number. Thus the two separate totals added together will always give the same overall total. It was out of these thoughts and conclusions that I eventually arrived at the trick *"Same Number—Same Card"*.

"*The Next Turn*"

This is a very straight-forward trick which depends for its outcome on disturbing the order of a sequence of cards. The secret of success with the trick is the ability to recognise the break of sequence which on occasions can be complicated. There is, however, a fool-proof system for verifying the out-of-sequence card. Take, for example, the sequence "3"—"2"—"Q"—"A"—"K"—"J"—"10"—"9"—"8"—"7"—"6"—"5"—"4". Begin with the Ace (A) and go either right or left to pick up the sequence "2"—"3"—"4" etc., ignoring any intervening cards. The card that is missing from and out of the sequence before you arrive back at the Ace is the selected card. In this example "Q" is the selected card.

Here are some further examples (the selected card is printed **bold**):

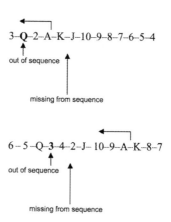

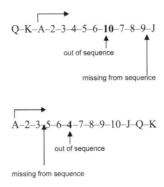

Q–K–A–2–3–4–5–6–**10**–7–8–9–J

out of sequence

missing from sequence

A–2–3–5–6–**4**–7–8–9–10–J–Q–K

out of sequence

missing from sequence

This trick is brought to a conclusion with what is know as "The Circus Trick", so called from its use by card-sharpers at fairs and circuses who gulled a spectator into making what he or she thought was a certain winning bet by offering to wager that "the next card turned over will be your selected card" when the spectator had already seen the selected card dealt out onto the table.

"You Can Find It"

It has already been observed in the "*Introduction*" that "it is surprising what can go unnoticed provided it is done boldly and the attention of the spectators distracted by directing it elsewhere". This trick has a number of examples of the very effective use of this technique to divert the attention of the spectator away from the handling of the cards by the performer.

At paragraph 7 of the description of the trick the spectator cuts the bottom half of the pack into two roughly equal packets. He or she is then involved in searching through the other half of the pack. This provides the performer with the ideal opportunity to arrange the cut-off cards in what is usually referred to as a false "cross cut" by placing the bottom packet of the cut on the packet that has been cut off, the top card of which is the card required by the performer. The deception is enhanced by the delay produced by the searching before the attention of the spectator is drawn back to the cut.

Another example can be found in the procedure for cutting the cards at paragraph 10 (1) of the description of the trick where again the requirement of the spectator to search for and count particular cards allows the performer to locate the required cards in the pack.